THE HALLMARK OF A GREAT LEADER

© 2021 by Martin R. Okumu

All rights reserved. This book or any portion thereof may not be reproduced or used in any manner whatsoever without the express written permission of the publisher except for the use of brief quotations in a book review.

ISBN: 978-0-578-89876-6

THE HALLMARK OF A GREAT LEADER

By Martin R. Okumu

The Hallmark of a Great Leader

© 2021 by Martin R. Okumu

The Author's professional credentials

Chief Information Officer – *San Francisco* – California – USA – https://sf.gov

The Johns Hopkins University – *Master of Science Degree* – USA – http://www.jhu.edu

Project Management Institute – Bay Area Chapter – *Coaching and Mentorship Circle* – California – USA – https://pmisfbac.org/

International Information System Security Certification Consortium – ISC2 – CISSP – *Certification ID: 431817* – USA – https://www.isc2.org

The Project Management Institute – PMP – *Certification ID*: *6033209* – USA – https://www.pmi.org

The Open Group Architecture Framework – TOGAF 9 – *Certified ID: 136203* – USA – https://www.opengroup.org/

DEDICATION

I wrote this book as a special dedication to my parents, my late father, Henry, and living mother, Anastacia, for their vision and lifetime investment in me. If not for their trust and faith in me, I would not be in this position. Special thanks to Heather, a legal attorney, and her partner, Mr. Johnson, for their trust in me when they hired me as a business partner and technology manager in their organization over twenty years ago. I want to thank the late Tom Kodula and his family as well as my siblings for their support and inspiration to pursue a business and technology career. I want to extend my gratitude to all leaders that believed in me by appointing me to positions of leadership within their organizations. Special dedication to my mentors, coaching staff, and my graduate and postgraduate professors. Many thanks to elected official Paul Miyamoto for the opportunity to lead a complex public safety local government organization in California. Finally, I want to thank my family and my wife, Judy, for her support, sacrifices, and guidance throughout the process. Special thanks to Elite Authors for their dedication and exceptional work in guiding the print while keeping me honest.

TABLE OF CONTENTS

Introduction ·ix

1   The Vision Hallmark · 1
2   The Leadership Hallmark · · · · · · · · · · · · · · · · · · · 9
3   The Social Intelligence Hallmark · · · · · · · · · · · 15
4   The Strategic Hallmark · 23
5   The Political Conscience Hallmark · · · · · · · · · · · 29
6   The Influencer Hallmark · · · · · · · · · · · · · · · · · · · 35
7   The Information Hallmark · · · · · · · · · · · · · · · · · 41
8   The Training and Formal Education Hallmark · · 47
9   The Emotional Wellness Hallmark · · · · · · · · · · · 53

Conclusion · 57

INTRODUCTION

Welcome to *The Hallmark of a Great Leader*. Throughout this book, I will reference the term chief information officer (CIO) because my career journey in business and technology radically sharpened my understanding of leadership and organizational effectiveness. I grew through the digital executive ranks, and it was through the CIO lens that I experienced my leadership journey to share with my audience and future leaders.

The Hallmark of a Great Leader will inspire and entertain you but, more importantly, keep you honest throughout your career as an executive. When I thought about writing this book, I realized that many of my CIO colleagues and C-suite executives struggled to navigate the complex web of corporate and executive leadership. I found this to be true for technology executives, but the leadership principles in this book apply to leaders in all sectors. *The Hallmark of a Great Leader* is an effective guide but not a bulletproof solution to all C-suite or career growth and development challenges. Readers will not find all leadership answers in this book or any other, but they will find nine hallmarks that can guide and inspire a CIO or C-suite executive to a greater path of success. I personally picked these hallmarks based on lifelong experiences and challenges in navigating the executive suite in the private and public sectors. If used together wisely, these principles trigger concepts that will prolong an executive's career while preparing you for a transition to the next career chapter. At minimum, I recommend learning three of the nine principles to achieve or experience success. Good reading and enjoy.

1
THE VISION HALLMARK

Without a vision, there is no direction. Without direction, there is no hope. Without hope, there is no faith, and without faith, there is no trust.
—Martin R. Okumu

A leader must have a vision. Vision is a cunning word used to lay out the direction of an organization. If adopted, the vision can become a powerful reality. Many of our American founding fathers had a vision of a "we the people" constitution. Martin Luther King Jr., an American civil rights activist, had a vision that white and black children would someday play together in harmony without fear and that one day people would not be judged by the color of their skin but the content of their character.

We know some visions have been realized and some have not, but they all have a constant theme—applying leadership skills to navigate adversity in pursuit of the ultimate vision.

As we delve into the vision narrative, I'll provide insights from the lens of a technology leader, but the principles apply to all sectors of leadership.

But why is vision so important to a CIO? You see, many CIOs join organizations and blindly assume the vision of the organization. While important, company visions are broad and play a larger role than the CIO. This is critical because CIOs miss the point and get tangled in the web of driving the company vision without realizing that the first thing, they should do is define their own hallmark vision for themselves and the people they lead.

But wait, Martin, how do CIOs define their own hallmark vision? An executive role is not managerial. If you are a CIO or an executive who does not understand leadership, things will get hefty fast for you. A CIO must define a sub-vision that they can align with the main company vision to realize the company's mission and objective. For example, a CIO should consider what they want to accomplish in their own role.

Remember that for successful CIOs, the role is not purely technical but requires influencing and guiding. In selecting your hallmark vision statement, you should be strategic while considering peer feedback. Examples of vision statements could be to "modernize our legacy mainframe in three years" or to "hire thirty women in technology by the end of the year." The CIO role is a leadership role; therefore, if you are not thinking about developing a vision, what's your purpose or value to the organization?

A leader cannot effectively help the organization ultimately realize its vision if they themselves can't formulate

THE HALLMARK OF A GREAT LEADER

a subvision. To align with the company CEO, the logic is simple. If your vision is to save the company money—say $3 million in twelve months—you already have the basic information to develop a strategic vision. If the CEO's vision is to have employees work remotely by 2030, and your subvision is to have the digital infrastructure in place to support the CEO's 2030 vision, the CIO and CEO of the organization are in alignment and are more likely to garner support from the top brass.

How does a CIO define a vision?

Before or after taking a leadership role, the first step is to define a subvision statement, and that involves studying the company's vision statement plainly printed on the company's website. If the company vision is unclear, the CIO should reach out to the human resources department for clarification. Once the company vision is read and understood, the CIO must align their personal subvision with the company vision. The vision should be written in bite-size, plain language and simple enough for the teams you lead to understand. No vision should be more than 150 words. After all, the CIO's job is to help the company achieve its strategic vision, not to introduce ambiguity or complexity.

As a word of caution, CIOs should never make the mistake of defining a vision that contradicts the vision of their organization. That's a surefire way to the unemployment office. Finally, the CIO subvision should be established quickly within the first ninety days on the job.

Once the vision statement is established, the vision must be socialized. The mistake many CIOs make is taking the first step to create the vision statement but placing the vision in a binder hidden in a cabinet. This is a mistake for the CIO. The vision should be readily accessible and referenced as CIOs navigate the executive leadership journey. CIOs should always refer to their vision statement as a reminder of where they want to lead the organization. If it helps, one recommendation is to create a vision statement visa card and carry it with you. The CIO can also request printed or digital vision statement banners to hang in the corridors or display on large monitors. If the CIO selects this path, they should consult with their human resources for clearance.

Next, once the CIO has successfully defined a subvision, the CIO should write a proprietary digital strategy plan if one does not exist. No CIO should plagiarize another company's digital plan. As a matter of fact, most plans are similar, but even then, it is a mistake to plagiarize. The CIO must remind themselves of their originality. One major mistake is that CIOs assume that they must write the top-of-the-line digital strategy within their first 180 days on the job. They quickly move to ask for million-dollar funding and mobilize resources to forge ahead with their digital strategy without assessing the current landscape. For example, is there an existing plan? Has the CIO read it? What changes are required? Are research partners involved? Instead, some CIOs rush to announce their desire to develop and publish a digital plan in the hope that the public relations buzz will accelerate the development of the plan. While this strategy may work, careers do not end well when technology executives and CIOs take this path. While creating anticipation and high expectations can lead to success, this strategy opens the door for pressure and failure. To avoid the chaos, CIOs should first draft their own original digital plan after spending their time reading and researching current projects and challenges both within and outside the organization. The CIO should then create a draft timeline—usually within ninety days on the job.

Once the CIO has developed a draft of the digital strategic plan, they should quickly move to create a plan of action. A simple tabulated word document populated with placeholder dates will do the trick.

Next, the CIO should schedule a checkpoint meeting with their boss or senior executive to present the draft of the subvision and digital strategic plan. This can be done via a Microsoft PowerPoint presentation. The presentation deck should be no more than ten slides. These presentations to leadership should be high-level. Stay away from the weeds.

After the CIO has scheduled the presentation, they should finalize the executive presentation. Remember, prior to this date, the CIO should have distributed the draft of their digital strategic plan. The executive strategic meeting should focus on the CIO's vision narrative and execution plan. In the slide deck, include information such as the request for the executive team and messaging to leadership, and remember, your boss or executives will always approach your presentations with suspicion and cynicism. It's your job to overcome these obstacles. Speak to your boss not as a salesman but with authenticity and sincerity. Don't be afraid to show a one-page cost-benefit analysis, a risk management page, and the value dividends.

Limit your presentation to thirty minutes. Executives do not give away their time freely. You must earn it, and make it count. It may be the difference between success and failure. Collect feedback during your presentation by allowing time for questions. You will have successfully completed phase one of sharing your vision by demonstrating to leadership how this vision aligns with the company. This presentation may also win you executive leadership champions in support of your vision.

Many CIOs do not follow this basic path. They move fast, build anticipation, and crash and burn quickly when the expectations are not met. These CIOs must backtrack to achieve buy-in and answer some tough questions, which—in my experience—never ends well.

The following list summarizes the steps CIOs should take to create and implement their hallmark vision:

10. Study the company vision, and create their own subvision statement.

11. If no strategic plan exists, draft a proprietary strategic plan emphasizing originality.

12. Identify a key executive who can help distribute the plan to key stakeholders for feedback.

13. Schedule a time to present the draft of your vision plan to your executives or leadership.

14. Develop your presentation.

15. Collect feedback.

16. Incorporate feedback as you move to the next phases of your vision and plan development.

Remember, as a CIO, your vision alone will not stand. With the help of your team's professionals and leadership approval, you will source professional services to benchmark your vision during the next phase. This will happen only after receiving an approval.

The successful outcome is important because three things happened. Leadership felt that your vision was in alignment with their vision; the investments to develop the next phases were reasonable because the CIO demonstrated that they understood the challenges within the organization, and the employees felt that leadership was on board.

After this, the CIO can return to take on the next ninety days of the plan. Next, let's discuss the powerful hallmark of leadership.

2
THE LEADERSHIP HALLMARK

You cannot buy leadership.
—Martin R. Okumu

Are leaders born or made?

CIOs and C-suite executives usually find themselves in executive roles by climbing the corporate ladder, applying for jobs, peer networking, or receiving executive appointments. In some cases, CIOs accidentally land in C-suite executive roles through political appointments with or without formal leadership training. Regardless of how the individual became a CIO, the soft skills of leadership must be part of a CIO's DNA. There are many definitions of leadership, but the one I coined is the ability to put oneself out of a job. In other words, a CIO should work themselves out of a job. But wait a minute—what do you mean by "work oneself out of a job?" You see, a CIO should empower and coach those they manage as a servant or transformational leader. Think of the CIO as a doctor. Doctors see patients, prescribe medication to heal, and follow up on patient welfare before taking on the next patient. The CIO's role is like the doctor's role in the sense that they empower those they lead to grow and become better future leaders. CIOs who fail to acknowledge this basic trait are bound to fail.

But how does a CIO know they have leadership skills?

Humans have debated leadership since the dawn of time. Is leadership inherited? Is someone born a leader? Is leadership contagious? Some expert scholars even suggest that some people are born with the leadership gene while others are groomed to become great leaders. We all can agree that there is not a single path to great leadership. The idea that you cannot buy leadership simply means that leadership is built on a foundation of life experiences and self-awareness accompanied by trials and tribulations.

However, there are paths CIOs can take to become effective leaders. The first thing a CIO should do is to learn their own leadership style. For example, there are several types of leaders, such as servant, authoritarian, transformational, or transactional. Ask yourself which type of leader you are. If you are unsure, ask yourself what type of leader you aspire to become. If you cannot answer these questions, you have no business being a CIO or C-suite executive.

As a matter of fact, you cannot lead if you lack self-awareness of your leadership skills. Fortunately, for many CIOs, the main objective of the role is to serve. The CIO role is far removed from power, money, fame, or prestige but more focused on strategy, direction, empowerment, and governance. It's about guiding and navigating a complex network of business processes, services, people, and compliance.

THE HALLMARK OF A GREAT LEADER

A CIO leadership role closely resembles the military. With the military, all missions are planned well in advance, and there is always a commander slated to lead the battalion to victory. A lot of planning and intelligence takes place, and training is never far behind, but one thing is for sure—the lead command embodies many soft skills pertaining to leadership, such as excellent communication skills, strategic thinking, a people-oriented mindset, and so on. Through coaching, training, and experience, the lead command ascended through the ranks to embody leadership qualities. CIOs follow a similar path, but no combat gear or guns are required. A CIO must plan, strategize, and execute while learning in the process. They must have the soft skills to lead large teams, companies, and projects to success. A commonality among leaders is confidence. They are willing to place everything on the line because they believe in themselves and their vision. Ask yourself the same question. Are you willing to put everything on the line because you believe in it? Great companies were born this way, but many also failed.

Leaders hide fear well and are known risk-takers. Leaders are prepared to face the consequences of their actions—good or bad—and never regret their actions. Some of the great leaders in our generation, such as Facebook CEO Mark Zuckerberg, Apple CEO Tim Cook, President Barack Obama, and Amazon CEO Jeff Bezos, have been fearless in their restless pursuit of their goals. They rallied millions of people to vouch for their ultimate vision and became successful in realizing their visions. We can take a page from these leaders because they had a vision, set goals, and rallied people to help them. As a CIO, you are in the same leadership role as these great leaders. You must think about the end and not how you will keep your job and benefits. It starts by having a vision and setting *smart* goals.

So how does the military example relate to a CIO role?

As a CIO, you have limited time to galvanize and exemplify leadership qualities. It starts by thinking big, creating a vision, and moving away from a myopic view. Someone once asked me, what is the difference between efficiency and effectiveness? An efficient CIO will not last in their executive role compared to their effective counterparts. Let me explain. An efficient CIO makes sure services, people, and processes are always on time, makes sure bills are paid on time, efficiently creates schedules, and always checks the box. While efficiency is an excellent attribute, many CIOs forget that being effective is key. An effective CIO already understands the day-to-day operations needed. They know people are assigned to roles to address efficiencies. They also know their time will not be well spent on developing efficient schedules or micro-processing. An effective CIO already knows the things that should be done. They channel their energy into being a trusted innovator and business partner (as opposed to a doer), breaking down walls to infuse new capabilities that add value to the bottom line, and fueling the growth of the organization.

What path can a CIO travel to acquire leadership skills?

They must first know the ins and outs of their business. Spend time studying your organization. The mistake that most CIOs make is to quickly implement new changes, replace employees, buy new products, and charter rush decisions thinking it's the rational thing to do. Take time to study the organization. This can take around twelve months.

Next, network with peers and participate in CIO roundtables. You benefit from listening to how other CIOs and tech executives interact. You gain a wealth of knowledge from their mannerisms, language, business, approaches, and strategy. If you do not play in this arena, you are missing out.

Think of yourself as a leader. Do not wait for someone to anoint you as a leader. After all, if you do not believe in yourself, no one else will.

Next, study other business leaders. Find a leader with leadership qualities that you admire or would like to emulate, and follow them on LinkedIn or other social media platforms. Your objective is not to be like them but to identify leadership attributes that make them who they are, and channel the experiences in your self-awareness.

Finally read, read, and read some more. I can't begin to tell you how critical this is. Find a leadership book and read. Read journals. Subscribe to blogs. If you are not a reader, try using audibles or enroll in leadership coaching classes, find a mentor or coaching circle, or watch leadership videos on YouTube to help grow your leadership bank.

The following list summarizes the steps you can take to become an effective leader:

1. Learn the business model.

2. Network with your peers.

3. Believe in yourself and develop self-confidence and self-awareness by practicing or reciting.

4. Find a mentor and study them.

5. Enroll in a leadership program.

6. Read, read, and read some more.

Let's now discuss the powerful principle of social intelligence.

3
THE SOCIAL INTELLIGENCE HALLMARK

Once words are spoken, the outcome is inevitable
—Martin R. Okumu

What is social intelligence?

Social intelligence is a soft skill every CIO or executive should aspire to have in their toolbox. It's not an obvious trait, but it plays a critical role in the development and growth of a C-suite executive. The term *social intelligence* resonates with the term *social impression*. If you are reading this book, you are familiar with how social media impacts people or companies with both positive and negative consequences.

Social intelligence is the ability to express oneself fittingly among business partners, family, friends, and competitors—and on social media platforms. It also means developing self-awareness and applying the skills in diverse business or social settings.

Some CIOs fail to capitalize on this element of leadership and fumble their approach to the CIO or other executive roles. I refer to leaders who fail to capitalize on social intelligence as the "Blinder CIO" or "Blinder Executive." Blinder CIOs function outside their executive leadership roles, solving menial tasks relegated to operations or management. In some cases, CIOs unknowingly gravitate toward their comfort zones—areas they were attuned to prior to getting the executive job. For example, a former data operator or GIS specialist in the CIO role may unintentionally drift toward their previous domain driven by comfort and experience. The biggest threat to this approach is that the executive is in a position of leadership or authority and may not guide their team to maximize their full potential or the vision. Think of the military example. A commander limited to a certain class of skills will have a challenging time leading the cavalry to victory.

Blinder CIOs or executives enter the job market with blinders on. When job hunting, they tend to review job boards and job descriptions and assume the executive tasks outlined by the employer should be completed sequentially. In some cases, organizations end up hiring these executives but fail to realize their mistake until it is too late. Sometimes Blinder CIOs assume a role because of the halo effect. The halo effect occurs when individuals are promoted to leadership roles because they are subject-matter experts. The hiring committee or managers make the mistake of assuming that subject-matter experts are leaders. The outcome is never

THE HALLMARK OF A GREAT LEADER

favorable to those being led and vice versa. In the end the organization takes the brunt of the loss for poor judgement and hiring choices. What these Blinder CIOs or Blinder Executives fail to realize is that they are their own brand.

Why is it important to realize or see oneself as a brand?

Technology is changing at the speed of light. A brand evolves to adapt to the market conditions. For example, we know what happened when companies such as Blockbuster faced off with Netflix. Another example is when Barnes & Noble competed with Amazon in the early 2000s. For many years, Blockbuster's strategy of brick-and-mortar stores was profitable, but in the early 2000s, the brand did not evolve with the consumer market of digital content streaming. While Blockbuster continued to sell content through DVD leasing and drop boxes, Netflix, born in 1997, seized the opportunity by investing in digital streaming content technology in partnership with established video streaming companies such as Roku. Netflix capitalized on the growing consumer market for fresh digital content and instant delivery. In the end Blockbuster lost millions of subscribers to Netflix, leading to its closure in 2010. Conversely, Amazon and Barnes & Nobles competed at selling books; however, Amazon expanded its services to retail and technology services. Today, Amazon is worth $314.9 billion compared to Barnes & Noble's $1.705 billion. Leaders who miss the basic concept of brand evolution will not be in their C-suite roles for long. In other words, if you are a Blinder CIO or Blinder Executive, through self-awareness, you should realize that being dynamic and challenging yourself to acquire the new leadership skills will serve you better for the long haul. The CIO must reinvent themselves.

To accomplish rebranding, CIOs and C-suites must channel their people skills, communication skills, and networking skills to improve business processes and operations while learning on the job. Mistakes happen, but social intelligence allows CIOs to capitalize on opportunities to learn and overcome obstacles and challenges. Social intelligence plays a tactical role in guiding the CIO throughout the business and professional terrain of executive leadership. CIOs should leverage social intelligence to communicate effectively and precisely. They must ensure that various stakeholders receive the information they need to advance business goals.

In some cases, social intelligence can be a CIO's worst enemy. For example, some CIOs or executives are outspoken and aggressive in their quest to pursue change or careers. In such cases, these CIOs lose touch with their role as a leader within the organization. They find themselves pursuing ulterior motives on social media or other platforms. This is where C-level executives must make smart decisions and air on the side of caution. We have read news stories about top executives being removed from their roles for sharing personal opinions contradicting their company values on social media. It's imperative to understand that an employer may not wish to associate their organization with your personal views, and doing so can lead to separation. As a CIO, always use social intelligence to air on the side of caution.

Intelligent CIOs know when to play their cards. They survey the landscape and audience and share relevant information pertinent to the setting. These CIOs or C-level executives leverage social intelligence hygiene, which means they research and maintain information balance to fittingly accommodate the setting or audience. I will be the first to admit that social intelligence may be the single most difficult attribute to hone or acquire, but a CIO can make progress through practice and research.

Leaning on a mentor or coach can always help the CIO or executive develop social intelligence. Another way to acquire social intelligence is to engage people in conversations through small talk. For example, start by learning about them by asking about their strengths and weaknesses, their hobbies, or their goals. Experienced CIOs with social intelligence often compliment others on their accomplishments—small or large. They know how to galvanize, organize, and rally teams through adversity. They accomplish these goals through social intelligence, and I can attest that a CIO or C-level executive who masters this art will find career success. As a side note, CIOs should never burn bridges or speak ill of their employer. Unfortunately, social media has made it simpler for well-trained executives to air their ill-advised grievances while on the job or upon separation from their employer.

There are no special courses for CIOs to train for social intelligence; however, through a combination of personal determination, training, and coaching, the skill can be honed. CIOs should understand that everything takes practice. It's also documented that some people are introverts, some are extroverts, and some are ambivalent. All CIOs should be able to adapt as leaders and use the military command example given earlier. As a leader, you cannot prepare for everything, but you can prepare for survival.

Being a CIO is not only about gaining exposure or developing your next project or product; it's about leading through communication, listening, and learning about people and their needs. You listen more than you talk. Although social intelligence is honed through experience, CIOs can consider a combination of classes or training programs to hone their social intelligence skills. Confidence builds courage, and learning from others is a surefire way to hone social intelligence.

The more you learn about the people you lead, the better off you are.

In conclusion, what can a CIO do to become better at social intelligence?

- Find a mentor or coach.

- Watch movies, and watch the actors; sometimes you will assume the role of actor in your role as CIO.

- Read relevant books on leadership and communication skills.

- Join social groups and roundtable discussions.

- Network like crazy—but wisely.

- Do not shy away from invitations. It's an opportunity to learn something new.

THE HALLMARK OF A GREAT LEADER

- Be genuine and authentic when speaking to people.

- Avoid coming across as manipulative.

- Be humble. Your title or credentials do not make you a leader.

- Use your leadership cape wisely.

- Incorporate formal communication etiquette and listening skills.

- Use your time wisely, and be selective how you spend it.

Next, let's discuss the powerful principle of strategy.

4
THE STRATEGIC HALLMARK

There is good and bad strategy.
—Martin R. Okumu

Strategy is a leadership trait that is vital to the survival of a CIO or C-suite executive. Whether you are an aspiring CIO or a seasoned CIO, you must be strategic in your ambition to drive change within the organization. In its simplest form, being strategic is the ability to codify information to create or add value to the business. A strategic CIO knows things that most CIOs don't. They use strategy in everything they do, say, or touch. Strategy can also be defined as a roadmap to a profitable outcome.

There are many classes, courses, and online articles that teach or speak to strategy; however, how you adopt and apply strategic concepts will make or break you as a CIO.

You see, strategic CIOs sift through layers of information quickly and then use the knowledge they gathered to make informed decisions. To them, strategy is their mode of operation. Some people assume that strategic people are manipulators. They associate strategy with ulterior motives, comparing an executive to a salesman trying to convince homeowners to buy something they already own. While there is some subtle truth in this, CIOs must be strategic because they will spend most of their time convincing others and negotiating to get what they need to drive their vision. Other than the 1 percent of CIOs working for *Fortune* 500 companies, CIOs will not simply walk into an organization and have the budget and resources they need to impact change or drive innovation.

A strategic CIO knows what's happening in the organization. They have a pulse on information in and out of the organization. I liken these CIOs to pit vipers' ability to sense infrared thermal radiations or bloodhound dogs' attributes to seek information. Some CIOs or C-Suite executives have the ability and experience to break down directives or information with ease. These CIOs are always on the offense and many times volunteer to solve problems, provide ideas, and lead with common sense. In some cases, CIOs can push their strategic agenda a bit harder than others with the same ultimate results. Sometimes this tactic can be dangerous for a CIO. A CIO who pushes strategy hard and crosses chasms may come across as arrogant and demanding while a CIO who sits back and waits for information and direction to arrive from the top faces the same fate. So it is best for a CIO to balance their approach in using the strategic hallmark principle to find the sweet spot.

THE HALLMARK OF A GREAT LEADER

How does a CIO become strategic?

It starts by knowing your audience. You must control your impulses when dealing with ranks of employees, businesspeople, and politicians. There is no such thing as knowing everything, but knowing when to manage your ambitious CIO strategic impulses can be beneficial to you and the organization.

You see, several years ago, I was in a board meeting to charter the next course for my organization. During the meeting, the CIO was asked a question related to the company's product line and their status on the development life cycle. The CIO used the opportunity to discuss technology in general while aggressively pushing for funding for projects that were on hold or not funded the previous year. Was the CIO wrong in pushing his agenda before the board? The answer depends, but in my opinion, he was being strategic after many of his tech meetings had been delayed or canceled for one reason or another. However, he was not strategic in recognizing his audience and the purpose of the meeting. Recall that we discussed the social intelligence attribute. The CIO picked the wrong audience to air his concerns. By simply responding to the question about the product line status, the CIO would have kept his seat at the table. Mistakes happen, and lessons are learned. A takeaway for CIOs and executives is to know your audience.

The second lesson is to know when and how to use strategy to get what you want. In the earlier example, the CIO's strategy did not work—not because he wasn't strategic—but because of poor judgement. Leadership is not glamorous, and mistakes happen. Learn from them, and move on. As a rule of thumb, never dwell on anything that happened in the past sixty seconds.

Next, to be strategic means doing research and staying informed about the business and the industry. CIOs who flourish have done their homework. They tend to know more than your average executive when it comes to business and technology. They study the industry and think outside the box. They speak in broad terms and use their vast experience to make sense of what's happening within their organization. Research takes many forms and does not require special training. You see, during your career, you will be bombarded with constant information. Your job as a CIO is to filter the noise and spend your time on what adds value to you and your organization. Spend time reading and researching solutions, people, and competitors, and stay informed. A CIO who is not informed will have a very short career.

Learn about your industry. Most CIOs forget to learn about things beyond their job and their role. The hallmark of a great CIO is wanting to know the ends of the industry they work in. They read materials and forge relationships with industry partners. They examine the direction of the industry and provide advice to their superiors on what's happening in the news as it relates to products and solutions.

Use succinct, clear communication. Many CIOs use jargon and buzzwords to excite their colleagues and partners and demonstrate their knowledge. They forget that the majority of the people they encounter do not care about the jargon and buzzwords. CIOs need to practice speaking in sales terms using simple yet effective communications

THE HALLMARK OF A GREAT LEADER

skills. Remove the buzzwords from business talk, and use simple, clear language. After all, your job is always to sell and achieve buy-in. If you constantly use tech-heavy Silicon Valley language, you may not be heard when it most matters.

Take a class. Most CIOs assume that they have reached the pinnacle of their career. As a result, taking a leadership class or training class is at the bottom of their to-do list. This approach limits the CIO from acquiring skills that may help them thrive in their role. Take a yearly or quarterly class on various leadership topics. These can be classes on team building, communication, or leadership.

In conclusion, what can a CIO do to become strategic?

1. Do research on various topics related to your work and industry.

2. Know your audience well.

3. Enroll in strategic thinking courses.

4. Use succinct and clear communication.

5. Learn about the industry you work in.

6. Share your experiences with colleagues, and look for feedback.

Next, let's discuss the powerful principle of political consciousness.

5

THE POLITICAL CONSCIENCE HALLMARK

Politics and business never mix, but they must work together.
—Martin R. Okumu

When referencing politics in this book, I am not referring to a campaign or running for political office. Politics in the context of this book means navigating adversity when business outcomes are driven by political ambitions. In some cases you may not have control of the business outcomes at all.

Let me explain. Unfortunately, like many leadership roles, CIOs are not exempt from politics. Some CIOs assume that their roles are immune because of their focus on ensuring optimal system operation, building new tech products, and driving large tech teams. This is a grand mistake. Fifty percent of the time spent in your role will be consumed by politics. Think about it. Most CIOs are hired or appointed through the ranks, and some go through brute job applications and interviews. Some arrive in their positions through networking. Regardless of how CIOs get their jobs, a similar scenario plays out behind the scenes. For example, some employees may constantly work to undermine the CIO's work because they think they have been passed for a promotion. Some employees may not like you, and usually this is true for all positions of leadership. In some cases, you may be caught up in difficult negotiations in business or other challenges within your organization. Either way, as an executive, you are in for a political fight—even though you are not running for office.

While these negative forces may be working against you, what can a CIO do to close the gap?

Being a great CIO demands that the CIO become politically savvy. Becoming political savvy takes guts and a thick skin. This means you should expand your role into activism. Why activism? Politics is a form of activism, and CIOs represent their direct and indirect reports the way government elected officials and representatives represent their constituents. In most cases, politicians are the same people who run certain factions of the organization, which means they may be your direct or indirect report. One easy way for a CIO or C-suite executive to gain ground in politics is activism. For example, volunteer with community or social programs that have nothing to do with technology. Participate in diversity programs or youth programs. You need to operate outside your CIO hat. This helps with a few things. You become diversified in your reach to nontechnical leaders and colleagues in your organization. You also expand

THE HALLMARK OF A GREAT LEADER

your reputation as just not a tech geek but someone who embodies organizational development reforms in all ways possible. It's unfortunate that most CIOs are not cut out for politics. Well, news flash: You better start thinking like a politician in your role if you plan to remain in the leadership role. Remember, you have to apply a combination of leadership traits to win. None of these traits can stand alone and have a great impact on your executive career.

Reach out to a mentor outside your organization. This should be someone who knows how to connect with the community and business—someone who has the complete opposite viewpoint from a CIO. They should not be a tech leader but preferably another business leader. If you choose to use a tech leader as your mentor, ensure they are a former tech executive with years of experience. They should have walked the ropes and learned a few things that could benefit you.

Another thing CIOs can do to overcome politics in the workplace is read and have an idea of what's happening with your unions if applicable. If your role is in government, follow the president, mayor, governors, and other city administrators and leaders on their work, such as voter registration, policy reforms, and other issues facing the immediate community. If you are in a private organization, make sure you know who your competitors are and what they are doing in your space. You should explore and learn about things like company products, revenues, markets, and expansion strategies. Make a habit of following your close market competitors.

You can also enroll in political classes. Not all of us do well in politics, but if you did not get a chance to attend business school or law school, you may want to take some political classes to learn how to better exert yourself in your current role.

Finally, be courageous, and don't be afraid to express your thoughts on issues. Courage is from the heart to the head. So no matter how much intellectual knowledge you have, your heart decides how courageous you are. Be brave. After all, weak leaders get run over quickly. You must face fear and be prepared to face the consequences—good or bad. Remember, everyone is dispensable, and you cannot hold on to anything forever. So what do you have to lose? If you play sides or "kiss ass" to keep your CIO or executive role, I can guarantee you that your career will not last long. CIOs must be firm and express their desire to lead and their position on issues within the organization. In doing so, make sure you do not overstep the boundary. Sometimes it's best to leave the dog fight if it doesn't concern you or your area of work. This is where the strategy hallmark compliments the politic hallmark. Moreover, sometimes you need to remind yourself that you are a CIO in a position of leadership.

In conclusion, what can a CIO do to become politically savvy?

1. Volunteer or engage in community activism.

2. Source a mentor experienced in politics, business, or other nontechnical field.

3. Enroll in political courses.

4. Use the strategy hallmark to compliment the political hallmark.

5. Be courageous and respectfully exert your position. Nobody is indispensable.

Next, let's discuss the powerful principle of being an influencer.

6
THE INFLUENCER HALLMARK

*As a leader, you should aspire to influence
not be influenced.*
—Martin R. Okumu

What's an influencer?

In this book we draw the term *influence* from a leadership perspective as opposed to the social media buzzword used to describe someone on social media with a large following.

To examine the influencer hallmark, let's begin by examining the roles of a manager and a leader to define the context.

What's the difference between a manager and a leader? Depending on who you ask, you will find different answers. A manager ensures that things get done. While this may sound untrue, 80 percent of CIOs who responded to our surveys fell under the roles of managers and supervisors. They just don't know it because no one likes to be classified differently than what they believe their role to be. The remaining 20 percent of survey respondents identified as tech or digital leaders.

I did a small experiment asking CIOs how they define their role as a CIO. An astonishing 70 to 85 percent deferred to managing technology and people, improving processes, and controlling budgets. As a matter of fact, many were so confident in their abilities as a CIO that they identified having no downtime, securing cybersecurity, and completing projects on time and under budget as the hallmarks of a great CIO. Another 20 to 25 percent responded that they were first and foremost business partners. This select group understood technology and knew the day-to-day operations were critical to the survival of their business but suggested that their role was far greater than that. They observed themselves as forward thinkers, helping the organization stay relevant and strategically assessing current needs and mapping them to future needs.

Regardless of how you perceive yourself, a successful CIO's true role is that of an influencer. Your role is to change how people think and perceive things within the organization by influencing their perception. As a CIO, you are being paid to think outside the box and drive new ideas into fruition. After reading the first few paragraphs, what type of leader do you consider yourself to be?

THE HALLMARK OF A GREAT LEADER

How does a CIO become an influencer?

Recall the hallmark vision discussed earlier. A CIO should have a vision to compliment the influencer hallmark. We discussed vision in the opening chapter of this book for a reason. As a CIO, you should have a big picture of how you plan to influence the organization. Far too often, CIOs walk into an organization without a plan. They focus on driving and executing existing processes that may add value from time to time. However, they fail to create that vision. Ask yourself what you would like to accomplish as a CIO for your organization.

Remember, I emphasized a vision because it becomes a compass for your future for the organization. Some CIOs assume that the business already has a vision for them, and therefore they just follow in line. If you are that type of CIO, you are in for a surprise. Let me remind you, having a vision for what you plan to accomplish for the organization as a CIO is a game changer. You must share that vision with management to gauge relevance and direction. If they buy into your vision, you have a winning strategy. You develop guardrails and a 90 percent chance of having a successful career. Your plan and vision will be the sounding board as you drive your execution strategy, release new products, or negotiate funding for programs and projects.

Far too often, CIOs have none of these plans. As a matter of fact, 60 percent of CIOs surveyed did not have a digital strategic plan nor did they know how to develop one. Forty percent wrote their own digital plan but did not know how to turn it into actionable items.

Developing and implementing a vision is a very difficult thing to do; however, to influence, you must have a CIO playbook and plan. This plan will help others champion your vision as you work through the roadmap. Remember, some people are good salesmen and can influence you using many techniques, but as CIO, you are in for the haul. You cannot apply sales techniques because the people you sell to—your managers and your employees—will start seeing the "horse crap." However, if you have a legitimate and genuine plan that addresses business needs, your job is cut out for you. Your leadership will bless your plan, and you can continue being an influencer, collaborating with teams to drive the common objectives.

Another way to become a great influencer is to learn the ins and outs of the business you are involved in. Know your leaders by name. Know the business stock performance. Know how many employees work for the organization—not just your employees. Know the numbers, issues, and challenges. Know your colleagues and business managers by name. Sometimes, just call to check in on a specific project or process. Remember, earlier I stated that you may become an actor in your CIO role. Some of the acting may require you to reach out to other sections of the business that you are not attuned to. The goal of playing an actor is like that of a salesman. You wear many hats to suit the conditions. Always remember the fundamental rule of leadership that not everything is intellectual or about technology; it's about the heart and connecting with people.

It's worth noting that as a CIO or executive leader, one thing that will kill your career right away is micromanaging.

THE HALLMARK OF A GREAT LEADER

This usually comes with a lack of experience or, in some cases, a lack of leadership skills. Many CIOs come up the ranks assuming that their role is to police all technology within an organization. Recall the Blinder CIOs? They attend all meetings, follow up on everything, butt into all email threads, call random meetings with little purpose, and lack trust in their colleagues to do their jobs. Is this you?

Are you familiar with such bosses or managers?

Of course. Let me explain. A micromanager will be evaluated based on the outcomes. They may receive high remarks for efficiency but poor results for effectiveness. Remember, you cannot lead without building trust. You must trust that business managers and employees can do their jobs. After all, some of them have been doing the same jobs for more than twenty years.

As a CIO, your job is to get out of the weeds and focus on empowerment. To be fair, some organizations are too small, and CIOs find themselves in the middle of the firefighting close to the line staff. Even if this is the case, CIOs should allow autonomy by creating a thriving environment. Your job as a CIO is that of a cheerleader. Allow for mistakes, then guide and correct with effective reinforcement.

Earlier I mentioned the term *empowerment*. This word is thrown around loosely, but as a CIO, you need to empower your employees. You give them the tools and protection they need to do their jobs. A CIO needs to influence how the employees work rather than creating roadblocks to progress. As an influencer, you job is to ensure that your employees also become influencers in their jobs in a positive light. A CIO who micromanages will eventually create dissent that leads to dismissal due to the politics that I mentioned earlier. A CIO must stay far but close—close enough to guide but not too far away so as to become an afterthought. It's a tight balance to create as a CIO. Recognize your role as CIO, and adapt. One thing to take away is to never micromanage and rather delegate tasks developing young minds. If you don't know if you micromanage, it's best to take a leadership class to help identify and correct the issue.

In conclusion what can a CIO do to become a powerful influencer?

1. Leverage the vision hallmark.

2. Learn the ins and outs of the business.

3. Never micromanage.

4. Empower the people you lead.

5. Create a balance between leadership styles. Don't lead by suffocation, but also be present.

Next, let's discuss the powerful principal of information.

7
THE INFORMATION HALLMARK

Everyone has information, but how you use and apply information is what matters.
—Martin R. Okumu

Why should a CIO have this hallmark?

As you already know, information is power. CIOs and executive leaders optimize how they access and use information. Information is bound to knowledge and research. It stems from ongoing personal and professional development and networking and through websites, blogs, search engines, and digital news. Information may be the difference between closing a deal, negotiating, or making key decisions in deriving value. If people are misinformed, the consequences can be detrimental. So why must a CIO be informed and have access to information?

As a digital leader, you will always compete against other companies, products, and talent in a global economy. Your organization will task you with providing business cases and contexts as they relate to projects, programs, and budgets. If you are ill-prepared, clueless, or misinformed, you will be rightfully doomed.

So what must CIOs do to remain relevant in their roles? CIOs need to seek information. CIOs and executives alike need to be hungry for information and passionate about the work they do. Passion drives the desire to seek information. If you find yourself lacking passion, chances are you are in a dead-end job. Leaders should go to networking events and attend digital roundtables to learn about different perspectives from colleagues and counterparts. A CIO sitting at their desk waiting for emails and direction from leadership will not be a CIO for long.

CIOs must be the aggressors not the "aggressees" if such a word exists. In simple terms, a CIO goes out of their way to forge a path of learning. They bring new perspectives to management and passionately discuss their sources of information. Nothing riles upper management more than an employee in a leadership role who fails to contribute to leadership discussions. Some CIOs, through no fault of their own, are wired to passively fulfill their day-to-day operations without contributing much to leadership. Some CIOs perceive their involvement in such matters as political. I touched briefly on the political spectrum in the previous chapter and explained how to leverage politics to your advantage.

One of the hallmarks of a great CIO is the ability to disseminate information. As a CIO, part of your job description is seeking information and knowledge. Once you have information, it behooves you to share the information with leadership and management. Some CIOs assume that the information they acquire is too technical for or irrelevant to management, but the opposite is actually true. Information is key because it helps with decision-making and situational awareness. It's your job as CIO to simplify the information for your colleagues in management, providing information they can quickly read and understand.

Let's be honest. Not all managers will be excited to see news and information from you, more specifically technology news. Make a habit of sharing information monthly or biweekly, and keep the information brief and appropriate for the audience. Nobody wants to sift through layers of information to find relevance in the message. For example, as CIO you learned about a cybersecurity breach in a competing industry through a colleague or virtual seminar. Should you notify your management team or leadership?

Well, of course, you should. It's your job to understand the nature of the risk and communicate it briefly, effectively, and clearly in a way a doorman can understand.

In other words, leadership will not care about threat vectors, threat indicators, or adversaries, but they will appreciate if you explain how the breach occurred and the impact it had on the business, product, or revenue. You must understand how to sell the message. It's not about gloating about your technical aptitude but more about selling information that could be useful in facilitating one of your unfunded security projects.

Let's use another example. Your organization downplays a solution that you have spent months or even years advocating for, such as multifactor authentication. Your chief financial officer always claims there is no funding to support the project. You could present the cybersecurity breach to management as an example of why investing in multifactor authentication is a good idea and explain how it can help the organization protect its intellectual property and crown jewels. This is one way a leader can get their projects funded, and you can clearly see the synergies on how information sharing and gathering can be your ally if used tactically.

Another avenue for CIOs to improve and strengthen their work is to learn from others. Some CIOs assume that once you reach the top of the totem pole, you are impervious to learning. This false narrative can jeopardize your success as a CIO. CIOs should operate as servant leaders when dealing with leadership. You should assume the role of CIL—chief information learner. You see, in your role, your job is to fully grasp the business and its operations. One way to accomplish this is by learning from others. You can benefit from listening to line of business managers (LOB) who have institutional knowledge and experience in their jobs.

Moreover, it will benefit CIOs to focus on learning about areas outside their comfort zones and using that information to find opportunities to advance the business or product. If you find yourself hanging out with your information technology colleagues, you should begin enterprising with the lawyers, the marketing team, or the human resources staff. Learn about and listen to their concerns. After all, you are a CIO because you rose through the tech ranks or were appointed to your position. Remember it's a win-win for the CIO and the business when both seek a partnership, but it takes a special CIO to seize the opportunity.

There is more information surrounding us in digital format than ever before. Smart CIOs identify relevant information and subscribe to blogs and technical digital subscriptions, such as CIO.com or govetech.com. The objective is not to spend half of your time learning about every piece of technology news that's published but rather to detect useful information that aligns with your personal and professional goals. I have come across CIOs locked in on information, feeds, and news outlets irrelevant to their career growth, development, organization, or industry. In other cases, executives become distracted by channeling their energy toward information that creates value for their hobbies as opposed to the interest of the business.

Finally, I can't mention information without communication. CIOs are supposedly busy individuals with limited time. While they attend meetings, review contracts, and make decisions while simultaneously managing teams, one thing CIOs don't do well is respond to emails. Electronic communication is the main communication channel between the CIO and their business partners.

CIOs who have assistants tethered to their desks responding to emails on their behalf can get away with managing their emails and calendars. For the 99 percent who still must manage the CIO workload along with their emails and calendars, make time in your schedule to read and respond to emails. Nothing upsets colleagues and partners like a CIO taking more than forty-eight hours to respond to requests. Sometimes the requests are not a high priority, but responding to the requester is a form of leadership. It's one way CIOs stay connected with the team. Some employees need personal interaction from a CIO, and email may be the only available avenue. Simple pleasantries can go a long way.

Some CIOs believe their position does not require them to respond to emails based on their rank or other factors. If that's you, you should reevaluate your leadership style.

To summarize, what should a CIO do with information?

1. Subscribe to digital information outlets on the web.

2. Learn from colleagues and partners.

3. Disseminate information relevant to the business.

4. Use information to sell and support your projects.

5. Be the aggressor; don't wait to be told what to do.

6. Always keep your boss informed.

7. Respond to electronic communication within twenty-four to forty-eight hours.

Next, let's review the powerful hallmark of formal training.

8
THE TRAINING AND FORMAL EDUCATION HALLMARK

You can use the same tools to do a job, but future jobs may not use the same tools.
—Martin R. Okumu

Why is this hallmark relevant to the success of a leader?

Education and formal training are not new to society. Scholars have long had their perspectives on education, and Americans of all backgrounds have their differences on how education and training should be administered. After all, the capitalistic nature of America allows anyone with or without formal training or education to be successful. A specialized skill can propel you to wealth and success.

Unfortunately, many Americans are unable to use their skills or talents to achieve a high level of success like entertainers, actors, or athletes, which brings us back to the value of having a college degree or higher education. Not everyone can afford a college degree, and not everyone has the luxury to attend college. However, through self-learning and brute-force determination, some individuals are very successful in their line of work as technology executives. Individuals have been elevated to CIO roles without higher education. While this happens, I must continue to emphasize how the job market for executive roles has been dominated heavily by individuals who have formal training and education.

If you search for a CIO position on a job-based social media platform, such as LinkedIn, chances are the job requires a master's degree and some formal certifications. These job qualifications can be argued in many ways, but the main objective is to sell the fact that anyone who has been through the rigor of a six-year training spree, coupled with several years of experience, is well suited to hold the technology executive role. Now, I am not going to argue with the bureaucrats on why this is the case, but the assumption is embedded in the job market, which makes finding a CIO job akin to finding a nugget of gold in the Rocky Mountains. You see, most individuals assume they are CIO material, but they are not. So the education merits do help curtail some of the wannabe CIOs.

Once they reach the pinnacle of their career, most CIOs assume that they have finished learning and training. After all, C-suite roles are executive roles, and they often assume that training or certifications are not necessary to remain competitive in their roles. If you find yourself in a C-suite role without any formal education, training, or certification, you should start investing in your education—no matter how good you are. I say this because when the separation happens—and it will, unfortunately—finding another executive job without any formal education will be challenging. It doesn't matter how many people you managed or how much money you saved the company, the next opportunity will be blind to your accomplishments. One way you can sell your accomplishments to another company is through your education qualifications. The modern resume-vetting technology allows companies to simply eliminate candidates that do not have an undergraduate or graduate degree; lacking education or training is a surefire way to keep your phone cold.

This brings me to certifications. Very few CIOs have certifications, but are certifications necessary? As a CIO, the answer is, blatantly, no. A CIO or C-suite executive can effectively do their job without having any certifications. CIOs are strategic people with soft skills as opposed to technical skills. Many successful CIOs running major global organizations and government agencies do not have a college degree, and some were dropouts from college. So, no, certifications are not required to become a CIO. However, the merits of being certified still play a role in job recruitment. Like having a college degree, certifications have become a standard for companies in their pursuit of filling executive roles. A CIO role is a sitting duck, and their tenure is usually one to two years with some managers spending up to five years in the role.

The threat to noncertified CIOs is that technology is changing rapidly. In reality, most CIOs have knowledge and experience on various technologies and are very efficient in posting their qualifications on paper, but if they lack certification, the job recruiting bureaucrats will use this loophole to hard-line your next job opportunity based on a certification. It could be the difference between getting a job and losing one to a less qualified candidate. You see, if you are a CIO, maybe you came through the ranks as a sales director, COO, CFO, or legal counsel. These careers do not require you to pursue any technology certifications. If you find yourself in a CIO role through these channels or appointments, make a point to complete some leadership technology certifications. For example, if you prefer to be a CIO for a security company, chances are that you should have some type of security certification. If you are a CIO who drives multimillion-dollar projects and product development, it may behoove you to have a project management or agile certification. If you are in manufacturing, a Six Sigma certification may help.

Some CIOs may scoff at the idea of becoming certified, which is entirely okay. You may have network connections or feel that finding your next job opportunity is not an issue.

For the other CIOs, having these certifications can reinforce their legitimacy as a CIO, especially when leading product and technical teams. If you can't speak the technology language, how can you translate business requirements into technology terms? Part of being a CIO is being versatile enough to speak to audiences of various backgrounds. A CIO should wear the transformational leadership hat when leading the business and directing its long-term strategic goals and the technology hat when conversing with technical counterparts and teams to drive innovation.

In defense of some of the CIOs, certifications cost plenty of time, effort, and money. It's unrealistic to set these expectations for CIOs riddled with busy schedules and never-ending workloads. Also, some CIOs come through other ranks without having a technical background, so to ask them to balance their duties while learning SDLC or the OSI model when they've never heard of the terminology is a long stretch. The best recommendation I can give a CIO is also one of the hallmarks of a great CIO—find a way to adapt. If the industry calls for a certification, plan to get it. Have faith in yourself and your ability because the certification processes are difficult and sometimes uncomfortable, but you did not become a CIO by snoozing. It took you many years to achieve the status, so becoming certified is one way to join the club and become competitive.

In conclusion what should a CIO do to achieve formal training and certification?

1. Enroll in a leadership class.

2. Align your training with the industry you work in and your future career plans.

3. Start with open certifications covering broad topics.

4. Invest in your college or postgraduate degree if you don't have one.

5. Seek a coach to help you plan and schedule your training and educational journey.

Next, let's brief on the powerful hallmark of emotional wellness and health.

9
THE EMOTIONAL WELLNESS HALLMARK

Your first breath of life is as good as your final breath of life. In between take care of yourself.
—Martin R. Okumu

Let's be honest. If you are not physically or emotionally healthy, you cannot be effective doing your job—or anything for that matter. Health and wellness should be common sense, but it's not as simple as the words sound. Although we care about our careers, profits, and ambitions, none of them can be accomplished without emotional wellness and well-being. For many CIOs, it may have taken many years to accomplish the feat of being recognized as a CIO. With leadership comes great responsibility. This means CIOs should exercise regularly and eat healthy. Body fitness leads to mental fitness, which means better productivity.

A CIO should also get regular sleep of at least eight hours per night and drink plenty of water. Being a C-level executive can mean many hours in the office and on the road. Use technology to organize your itinerary, and never be afraid to take a mental day or time off. If your employer has issues with you taking time off to heal yourself, your body, and your mind, you should find another job. Never, ever apologize for taking care of your health or your family. If your work-home balance is diminished because of your job, start looking for other opportunities. Working yourself to the emergency care unit is not worth it. After all, someday you will need your health to enjoy everything that you have worked so hard to accomplish.

Treat your body as a temple, and nurture your brain cells. Take walks, watch a movie, and spend time to build your spiritual capital. Find inner peace so that you can lead others to prosperity.

In conclusion what can a CIO do to maintain emotional health and well-being?

1. Exercise frequently.

2. Drink water.

3. Take mental days off.

4. Eat healthy.

5. Join a peer support group.

6. Plan for annual physical checkups.

7. Spend time with your loved ones.

CONCLUSION

The CIO or C-level job is a prestigious role. It can take many years, good health, and some luck to ascend to the pinnacle of technology. It's well documented that the CIO role has evolved over the past decade. The role of the modern CIO is no longer about keeping the lights on or delivering projects on time and under budget. The modern CIO is consistently challenged by the competitive market and never comfortable in their role. CIOs never stop learning!

This book, *The Hallmark of a Great Leader*, by Martin R. Okumu, shares real-life experiences and leadership traits that seasoned technology leaders or aspiring technology enthusiasts can use to become a CIO or ascend to the pinnacle of their careers. Education and certifications are not the answer to becoming a successful CIO. It takes all the principles and hallmarks in this book to be an accomplished CIO.

If you are not a CIO but aspire to become one, you must work on your soft skills and formal education and training. If you are lucky to have a CIO in your organization, reach out to them for advice, and find out how they became a CIO. In my own experience, I had to compete on brute-force job applications to win the roles in my career. Not a single time did I get a role because I knew someone. This is different from someone being appointed to the role because they worked in the organization for years, knew someone in the organization, or received a referral for hire by a close friend or colleague.

Conversely if you are already a CIO, think about your next role. Do you want to continue as a CIO, or do you aspire for something else? In my opinion, CIO and C-suite roles are not long-term roles because at the C-suite level, politics supersede technology success. So at some point, politics will eventually disrupt the role. When that happens, have you checked your formal list we discussed briefly? For example, do you have the formal education and industry certifications? Do you have a professional resume? Do you update it frequently? Are you continuously learning? If you don't start preparing, making the $100,000 to $500,000 per year may not come as easy as you thought in your next opportunity. That's why *The Hallmark of a Great Leader* is an excellent book to read and learn from. It's factual and calls it like it is.

Thank you for the support and for reading my book. I hope it will guide you to a successful and prosperous career.

www.ingramcontent.com/pod-product-compliance
Lightning Source LLC
Chambersburg PA
CBHW070209100426
42743CB00013B/3109